Scrum Tales

Stories From a Scrum Master's Diary

Jimmy Kidaram

ISBN: 1514160943
ISBN-13: 9781514160947

Dedicated to all the Scrum teams I have
worked with.

Let's Keep It Simple.

CONTENTS

Preface

Preface

About this book

Scrum is a lightweight framework that is easy to understand but difficult to master. The journey from understanding Scrum to mastering it is interesting. We experiment and learn at every step of this journey. We will be debunking many myths at various stages of this journey. We will learn not only from our experiences but also from the experiences of others. We will encounter numerous interesting scenarios during this journey, which have served as learning opportunities; this book mentions a few of them. These scenarios are small incidents, comments, and perceptions picked up from their place of origin. Each scenario is analyzed within the Scrum framework.

A basic knowledge of Scrum is desirable, but not mandatory before reading this book. This book addresses different needs simultaneously, which will provide a better understanding of Scrum to anyone associated with it. A Scrum Master can relate these topics to his day-to-day experiences. A Scrum Coach or a Scrum Trainer will gain ready-to-use examples. This will help in answering many situational questions on Scrum.

Acknowledgements

This book has some references taken from the Agile Manifesto and principles behind the Agile Manifesto. The Agile Manifesto is available at http://agilemanifesto.org and the principles behind the Agile Manifesto are available at http://agilemanifesto.org/principles.html. Please have a quick look at these.

The content used in this book references the Scrum Guide, which was developed by Ken Schwaber and Jeff Sutherland, and maintained by Scrum.Org and ScrumInc. The Scrum Guide is available at http://www.scrumguides.org.

1. Keep It Visible

"James, we have a situation on hand!!!!!," Susan ran behind James to stop him in the corridor.

Susan has taken up the role of the Scrum Master recently and maintains a great rapport with James, another Scrum Master in the organization.

"We are in the middle of the sprint. John was on leave for a few days in the first week; we have considered this while planning, but he forgot to add his tasks for the second week in the tracking tool. Now if we add it, it will create a burn up"

"So what is the problem?" James was quick in his response, but Susan was not in a mood to listen; she continued with her proposed solution.

"We will add his tasks in three small batches; we are expecting good burn downs during the next three days; therefore, the impact won't be visible."

This may seem like an exaggerated example, but can occur in new Scrum teams because of many reasons including lack of Scrum knowledge, wrong coaching, and the surrounding Scrum-but organization.

This is a question on transparency as perceived by the team. Why should we hide a problem? Problems provide us with an opportunity to inspect and adapt. Let the problems be visible so that we can address them the next time.

Why is the team worried so much about burning down tasks than creating value? They are missing the fundamental concept that the sprint backlog is a live document, which will keep changing throughout the sprint. The development team has complete authority to change it. If they feel that their initial estimations are incorrect and there is a risk associated to the sprint goal, they can negotiate with the Product Owner.

The team has become more "burn-down" driven than "value" driven. The executing organization may be responsible for this behavior. There may be a huge pressure on the team to report in terms of burn down in hours. This causes the team to concentrate more on burning down tasks than on creating value. Many teams continue to try to list down all the tasks for a sprint and recalculate them every day to produce a true burn-down chart. Scrum Masters may fail to protect the team from the pressure to create a fully formed sprint backlog on the first day itself.

It is time to switch focus on the fine graining of user stories and tracking progress based on these stories. We should understand the trade-offs and our specific situations and take a call. However, there is nothing wrong in analyzing our practices to understand if there is a "waste" in recalculating and tracking in terms of hours within the sprint.

2. Un-Title Ourselves

"We don't have sufficient testers in our team. It is a complex application that needs extensive testing with several scenarios."

How many times have you heard such a statement? I am sure it has happened at least once. I remember going to an office to get an official document; I had a tough time in getting the document ready. The real obstacle emerged later. The officer who was supposed to hand over the document to me was on leave for two days. The only task for him was to make an entry in a register kept near the exit and get it signed from me. No one else was ready to perform his task because they didn't want to interfere with someone else's job. It was a silly reason. Does this type of red tape exist in our teams?

Do we still work as different units? Are there testers, developers, analysts, and so on? How long will it take for us to overcome this and start working as a cross-functional, self-organizing team without any titles? Scrum doesn't recommend any titles within the development team. All members are development team members. We will have specific capabilities; we will be specialists in some areas, and this is not a concern. However, this should not create any boundaries around us. A team is cross functional and each member should simultaneously try and develop cross-functional skills. I can continue working on my area of expertise as it is the area where I can yield best results. However, simultaneously, I should be available and ready to be involved with other aspects as well if the situation demands. In simple words, I should do the work that the team requires at the moment.

How can we address the situation stated in the beginning? One way can be what we have discussed so far and that is to emerge out of the constrained mindset of titles. Another way to approach the problem is from an automation angle. We should automate the test as much as possible so that we save time in testing. This will help in the cross-functional way of working. Any member will be able to execute the test cases and it can be done more frequently.

3. Divide and Conquer, not Split and Claim

Many times when we implement new Scrum projects, there will be many interesting characters around us. There will be people to support the transformation from organizational and management perspectives. However, at times they volunteer for some additional contribution. They may be doing it with an intention of helping us. However, we should ensure that unlawful practices are not introduced into the team during such instances.

A team new to Scrum was running their first sprint. Several concerns arose during the sprint because of factors such as lack of Scrum experience, failure to identify dependencies in advance, and changes in requirements. It was a chaotic situation. The team was developing the increment but was not in a position to meet the done criteria for any of the stories. They were inspecting each mistake and was confident of putting up a good show in upcoming sprints. The Product Owner decided to continue with the sprint even though no increment was obtained from it. The sprint was two-week long and whatever parts that the team completed would be valuable as inputs for the next planning. Everyone was extremely optimistic even in this situation and looking forward to the next planning session.

The savior, the manager who was keeping a close watch on all these developments, enters the scene.

"I have a formula to pull you out of this situation," he was prepared to play a cameo.

"We will split each story in to two parts: what is done and what is not done. Whatever we have done will be considered as the output from this sprint and the rest will go back to the product backlog. This will help us save face and we can claim that we have produced an increment in the first sprint itself."

The intention is clear here, but it is a wrong practice. What should we do if we fail in a sprint? Accept it first and then inspect it. Scrum maintains higher levels of transparency so that the concerns are identified at the earliest and the team will get an opportunity to correct them. It is recommended to start the first sprint as early as possible so that we can resolve the concerns as early as possible. We should not try to manipulate and cover up failures.

Displaying high velocity should not be the reason for splitting the user stories. In addition, the middle of the sprint is not the right time to do that. If the team detects some problems with the committed scope, it should approach the Product Owner. The team can renegotiate the scope with the Product Owner without affecting the sprint goal.

4. Are We Ready for the Sprint

What should be the inventory levels in the product backlog? How many stories should be ready for implementation at the beginning of the sprint? An immediate answer can be more than what can be accommodated in the upcoming sprint. As we have discussed, the development team works in cadence. The rhythm will be disturbed if the team doesn't have enough inputs for the planning.

"You start with these items; during the sprint I will give you a few more. Put some placeholders for those items."

We might have heard some or the other version of the preceding statement. The product backlog has so many items but few are ready for implementation. The Product Owner tries to groom items within the same sprint. Another aspect of the same problem can be observed in the form of unnecessary items in the backlog. Just because we don't have sufficient items, new items are created. It will take the form of a proof of concept for some features that never come, an irrelevant nonfunctional concern, and so on. All these are done to ensure that the team is engaged. We create an unnecessary burden for the team, in the attempt to cover up the root cause: lack of refined product backlog items.

We should now address the real concern, that is, availability of product backlog items, which is the responsibility of the Product Owner. The Product Owner should effectively divide his time among the stakeholders, grooming tasks, and the team. The development team can help him in this activity using up to 10% of its time. However, the responsibility remains with the Product Owner. Many good practices exist regarding the inventory levels within the product backlog. Many teams consider it a rule to maintain groomed items sufficient for the next two sprints. This provides a more efficient control. If we observe a downward trend in the ready items, we will have sufficient time to react to it.

Now what can be done if we don't have sufficient items at the beginning of the sprint? We will plan only those items that are ready for implementation. The concern should be identified so that we can inspect and improve on it. Don't cover it up with dummy items. Should we take more items in the middle of the sprint? The Product Owner can negotiate with the team to include more items if space is available. However, a risk is associated with this. The new items and even the existing goals may face problems. The Product Owner is responsible for directing the team. If he is aware about this risk and ready to accept it, we can go ahead with the addition. This is only if the team is ready to take up new items. However, this should be an extremely rare case, not an everyday practice.

5. Nothing More, Nothing Less

We were working on a customer UI for registering complaints. It was a simple UI and the user story had all the required details. But it was found that the work was not progressing as expected.

"Are we facing any issues?" The Scrum Master had a gentle query.

"Not like that," the team answered. "We are trying to implement auto completion capability for the screens."

"Is it part of the user story?"

"No, but the Product Owner will be happy to see this proactive step from our side."

Key words, such as value addition and providing some additional value to the customer, were usually heard in offshore development centers a few years back. Attempts were made to increase customer satisfaction by providing them something more than what was promised. However, in such attempts, do we fail to provide what was promised?

Please carry out an Internet search to find out the following figures. What percentage of software projects is successful in delivering the promised value to the customer? What percentage of the features that we develop is really useful? The results will make us change our perceptions.

How much work should we complete within the sprint? The answer is simple: only that much what we have decided during planning and promised the Product Owner. It is good to propose innovative ideas. We should share them with the Product Owner. If required, he will create a separate story for that. He is the person responsible for maximizing the value that the team produces. Our suggestions may provide value to the end user, but there will be items that are more important to the customer. The Product Owner will be able to offer correct direction. Therefore, we should convey our ideas to him and let him decide the next step. Our aim during the sprint is to complete the sprint goal as committed during sprint planning.

6. The Incremental Review

"I don't want to see these dead screens. Call me when it is functional." This was a reply from a customer to an invitation for reviewing screens for a new functionality that was being developed. We wanted to receive an early feedback for the screens that we were developing. The Product Owner wanted to take these screens to a large audience for receiving feedback. However, the stakeholders were not ready to view these screens in bits and pieces; they wanted to review them together.

This situation has many aspects. Let's first approach it from a stakeholder's perspective. A stakeholder has the right to express his opinion. He may be from the old school of thought where requirements are thrown over the wall. He has the Product Owner and has conveyed all his requirements to the Product Owner and given him the freedom to choose the best for the business. Then why does the stakeholder get disturbed every now and then? All this sounds fine until we read the following principle:

"Business people and developers must work together daily throughout the project."

So what can be a more optimistic scenario? Business should not be affected often and simultaneously we should ensure effective collaboration on a daily basis. The key person here is the Product Owner. He is the single source of requirements and should be capable of validating the increments that the team produces. However, this doesn't reduce the responsibilities of other stakeholders. They should provide the required support to the Product Owner.

The Product Owner should possess the highest level of knowledge regarding requirements and the business value that they provide. He should negotiate and obtain sufficient time from stakeholders to support his activities. He should ensure that stakeholders appreciate the incremental way of delivery. He can take help from the Scrum Master in developing this agile mindset.

The Product Owner should simultaneously optimize the time that is provided by stakeholders. It is a good practice to conduct incremental reviews with stakeholders. However, it should not be too frequent. The Product Owner, with his product knowledge and understanding of the business should be able to handle such reviews to a certain extent. At the same time, the stakeholders should understand the agile way and should be available for the Product Owner.

7. Time to Deliver

"What have you done during the last two weeks?" The delivery head asked the Scrum Master when he entered the delivery head's cabin. He was summoned for a quick meeting on a Monday morning. The staging application was displayed on a computer and the manager's eyes kept moving quickly from the monitor to the Scrum Master's face.

"I am not seeing any increments to the application. Does it mean that you did not work during the last four weeks?"

"Yes, we are doing better work," the Scrum Master tried to explain. "We are working on a large capability, which will take one more sprint to complete. It is expected to be in staging within the next two weeks."

"But do you know what Scrum demands?" The manager got in to his coaching shoes. "Our aim is to deliver working software every sprint." This happens when we begin learning any new philosophy. We always tend to go by the words rather than understand its concepts.

An organization will take some time to understand what agile is and what it is not. We encounter many such personalities during our journey. Scrum produces a potentially shippable increment in every sprint. However, the Product Owner decides whether to ship it or not. His decision will be influenced by many factors including the current state of the feature, value that the current increment carries, and holding costs against deployment costs. Based on many such factors, the Product Owner decides what to ship and when. Many considerations, such as minimum marketable feature and minimum viable product, are taken into account.

However, this does not stop the teams from delivering potentially shippable product increments. The development occurs in cadence. However, the delivery depends on many factors. The Product Owner may decide to ship the increment as it is or waits for further enhancements before deploying it.

A Scrum Master has to play the role of a coach here. He is responsible for supporting the agile transformation in the organization. The Scrum Master should ensure that the Scrum way of delivering value is understood and imbibed by the team.

8. The Plan that Emerges

"Do you know the planned utilization of the team for these two weeks?" Scrum Master was facing this question from the Delivery Head. "It is less than 40%."

"No way," the Scrum Master replied. "We have enough user stories taken up for this sprint. Actually we were not able to accommodate all stories proposed by the Product Owner."

"Look at this," the manager supported his argument with evidence. "You have informed me that you have completed the sprint planning. The total tasks planned for these two weeks are nowhere near the capacity."

The manager was referring to the tasks created in the sprint backlog. He had calculated the total effort for all tasks listed in the sprint backlog. I can recollect many occasions where I got strict instructions from the management to list down all the tasks on the first day of the sprint. The argument was that it is a two-week sprint. Why can't we have a detailed plan for a short duration?

I prefer to take a moderate stand here. Of course, I don't agree with the argument that the complete sprint backlog should be in place on day one. At the same time, I can't say it is not a valid question. What are we supposed to do? We have the proposed items for the sprint. We have decided on the sprint goal and a plan on how we are going to achieve it. Once these are in place, we will decide the tasks for the first few days of the sprint. We may be unable to predict all the tasks as work will be added when we start sprinting. As and when we receive more clarity, we will keep updating the tasks in the sprint backlog. A sprint backlog is a live document, an emerging artifact that is owned by the development team.

I have worked with many successful teams who don't even worry about the minute-level tasking or listing down using a software tool. They prefer to deal with small user stories and track their progress based on these stories. However, can we recommend this for all the teams? What will happen if the team is new to Scrum? The team should bring in some additional level of control for themselves. It doesn't mean that we should list down all the tasks on day one. However, for new teams, listing down all known items on day one itself will be helpful. We have all the right to change them later in the sprint if our assumptions go wrong. This inventory will help them in looking back and determining ways to improve in the future.

Irrespective of the level of details that we are maintaining in the sprint backlog, it should enhance our sprint goal. It should not create an additional burden or roadblock in creating and delivering value, that is, the goal of the sprint.

9. The Right Mixture

What is the ideal size of a Scrum team and how should it be structured? I received this query from one of my friends who was preparing for an interview. I told her that it should be between three and nine. If it is less than three, accommodating all the capabilities required in the team is difficult. If it is more than nine, proper coordination is difficult. However, how do we choose a number?

Scrum mentions cross-functional and self-organizing teams. Self-organization is a challenge if we have a considerable number of team members; also, it is difficult to form a cross-functional team with extremely few members. Therefore, the ideal choice will be a number between three and nine with which we can accommodate most of the capabilities required for a team.

I remember a situation where the team structure was being discussed. A lot of effort was spent to strike a balance in various aspects. They were trying to maintain a balance regarding project experience. Several combinations were discussed to ensure that all the capabilities were present in all the teams. They concentrated on the gender ratio as well. However, one important point that was missing was what kind of work each team was going to take up.

Why do we have Scrum teams? Scrum teams deliver a shippable increment of the product in every sprint and the structure of the team should be based on this. The starting point of any discussion regarding the structure should be to understand the expected output from the team. Even within the same project, there will be teams working in some specialized capabilities such as end user applications, web service interfaces to be exposed for other systems, integration with social media, administrative tools, and so on. The required capabilities will differ based on the area on which the team is focusing.

It is not just a number-crunching exercise to arrive at an optimal team structure. We should consider all the factors including agile aspects. We should be able to identify possible risks regarding team cohesiveness and individual constraints. Teams should be structured in such a way that the benefits of agile and self-organization are maximized.

10. Finish to Start

We once again review the biggest timeboxed event of Scrum, that is, sprint. What can be the maximum duration between two sprints? I remember the first Scrum team that I had worked with. We had kick-started iterations and completed two sprints. However, the third sprint started only after three weeks. The team was dragged in some other activities. It was involved in creating patches for some other application that it was working on before. Even during the next few sprints, many members switched between these two products.

Many such instances can be found related to this. We will discuss a few of them here. We have completed a couple of sprints and identified areas that need improvement. Why can't we stop for a few days and attend some training to enhance our capabilities? Another reason can be the upcoming holidays. Because of many holidays in the next two weeks, the availability of team members will be less. Why can't we begin afresh after the holidays?

Even though not very common, some antipatterns exist that include buffers between sprints. We might have heard some comments such as "Let's not have a release sprint. Instead, we will put a week buffer after every fourth sprint. This can be used in many ways, such as a buffer, time for training, and fine-tuning of the product."

All the aforementioned factors are smells that we must get rid of. The Scrum team should focus on its tasks and be dedicated to the results. In unavoidable cases, resources can be shared, but remember it will have an impact on the self-organizing capabilities of the team. We can reserve some time for trainings and building capabilities within the sprint. We can calculate our capacity based on the availability. This should not be a reason to stop the sprints.

Holidays should be considered when we check our capacity during planning and plan based on availability. We should not keep technical debts to be addressed during buffer time. Each sprint should produce a shippable increment. No concept of buffer periods exists between sprints.

In simple words, the next sprint starts the moment the previous sprint ends.

11. It is Our Plan

"Please check your mail," a voice came out of the account manager's cabin, followed by a smiling face. We were about to start working on a new product.

"I have sent you the list of items that we have to complete in the first two sprints. I guess this is enough for you to start. We will add to it as we progress."

"But we have a Product Owner, right?"

"Yes, we do. We had a meeting with the Product Owner and other stakeholders and created this list. Don't worry; he will be creating the user stories in the tool by the end of the day."

This is an unwelcome situation. I don't think anyone will agree to what we have heard just now. So without analyzing its merits, let's see what can be a better situation.

For anything related to requirements or business direction, we need to turn to the Product Owner. His duties are broadly divided in to three parts. Collaborate with all stakeholders to understand the requirements, create and maintain the product backlog, and collaborate with the development team. The third item includes effective communication with the development team on the requirements, being available for support, and accepting or rejecting the work. It is only the Product Owner who provides requirements to the team. No one else, not even the big shots in the hierarchy, hold any rights to do this.

Now, who decides what should be done in a given sprint and when? The Product Owner creates the backlog, prioritizes it, and refines it with the help of the team. The team estimates the items in relation with one another. The Product Owner clearly communicates the business priorities and his expectations from the sprint. Based on these priorities and the available items, the development team decides what best they can do in the upcoming sprint. They discuss this with the Product Owner and make adjustments based on the negotiations with the Product Owner. Finally a decision is made on the sprint goal and the team explains the strategy by which it is going to achieve it.

In short, the Product Owner is the only role who communicates the requirements and their priority to the team. The development team and Product Owner decide the sprint goal. The Product Owner's decisions represent the stakeholder's expectations and will be influenced by the aspirations of the development team. The decisions from the development team will be in line with the business priorities set by the Product Owner. This synergic coordination ensures a smooth working model.

12. The Magical 15 Minutes

"Tom, let's call Stephan and get it finalized?" John was about to dial Stephan while asking this question to Tom.

Tom and John are part of a Scrum team at an offshore development center and Stephan, their Product Owner, is working from a different location. They have some questions about the story that they are working on.

"Hold on, John," Tom replied. "Why are you in a hurry; we have the daily scrum at 10 AM and we will discuss this during that time."

However, John had another idea. "But Tom, I will be having a discussion with our Infra team during that time. I may be joining only toward the end of the daily scrum to share my updates."

This is an extract from a conversation held among members of a newly formed Scrum team. We can observe many such instances particularly with new teams.

Why do we conduct daily scrums? A scrum is an "inspect and adapt" event. There are release, sprint, and daily plannings. A scrum contributes to the third level of planning, that is, the daily plan. The "three questions" provide a perfect format for this event. Many times, as required, team members regroup just after the daily scrum to discuss concerns and decide in detail about the action to be taken in the next 24 hours.

To answer Tom, a daily scrum is not a requirement clarification session or meeting for problem solving. He shouldn't wait for the daily scrum to get his doubts resolved. Remarks regarding requirements and other concerns may influence the three answers that the team gives. However, it should not initiate a long discussion. If a long discussion is required, concerned members should meet, may be soon after the daily scrum and discuss.

To answer John, team members should be present throughout

the event. This is not just for sharing your updates with the Scrum Master or Product Owner. In Scrum, we commit, succeed, or fail as a team. We should be aware of what is happening in the team and contribute to its success. We shouldn't plan any other parallel meeting during the daily scrum.

13. Refine the Refinement

When we move from a conventional waterfall approach to Scrum, we go through many interesting phases. Looking back on our early days with Scrum, we can recollect many such stories. We can recollect mistakes with a smile on our faces, such as those from our childhood.

I remember the first backlog refinement session conducted by a new Product Owner. The team and the Product Owner were new to Scrum. Because of the training that he underwent, the Product Owner did a good job in fine graining the user stories and detailing them as much as possible. He had scheduled a refinement session on a Friday afternoon.

"We have 10 stories that we can take up for refinement. I have ordered them based on their priorities. So we will try to groom the top five today." The Product Owner was setting an agenda for the session. However, his next sentence was a killer. "But first, let's quickly estimate all 10 of them and put some tentative dates against each."

Team members were at different levels of understanding of Scrum and many eyebrows were raised at this statement.

"Don't you think it is too early to do that?" the Scrum Master joined the discussion. "We don't have stories in the ready state. We are yet to do a relative sizing. We can make such predictions later when we do a planning."

However, the Product Owner had his own constraints as he had to communicate tentative delivery dates to the business. For the business, these dates served as indicators for their plans.

How can we solve this problem? Do you agree with the statement given by the Scrum Master? This problem has two major dimensions. What is the intention of the grooming session? How can we address the business need?

In simple words, the refinement or grooming sessions are conducted to create and maintain a good product backlog. The Product Owner explains the backlog item(s) and the discussions result in an improved item(s). During this process, we write backlog items, split or merge them, remove the items, reorder them, detail them further, and perform a relative sizing for them. At times, some antipatterns creep into this meeting and it becomes a proxy planning session. Scrum doesn't prescribe this meeting as a formal ceremony. However, it has its benefits and intended output: an improved product backlog with more items in a ready-to-implement state. We should not try to club activities from the planning session to this session.

The business will obtain a clear picture only once an item goes through the planning session, and only if the item is added to the sprint backlog. However, this remains a speculation based on the team's current velocity. Can the business people get a little more visibility on the future plans? The answer is yes; this can be achieved using the next higher level in the planning called release planning. We can achieve it at an epic, a feature, or a user story level based on our requirement hierarchy, state of product backlog, or best practices that the team follows.

However, the bottom line is that a plan is based on predictions and a certain amount of uncertainty is involved in it. It is a speculation based on what is known today.

14. Time Your Plan and Plan Your Time

Timeboxed events are prescribed by Scrum to regularize and avoid unnecessary meetings. This doesn't mean that there should not be any other meeting other than the prescribed ones. These prescribed meetings have some reasons and defined goals. We should not skip any of these meetings. Avoiding any of the prescribed events will prevent us from receiving the benefits of Scrum. Scrum exists in its entirety.

I have overheard a Scrum Master saying that we have already decided on the user stories for the next sprint during our refinement sessions and we don't need a planning meeting now. We can determine more than one antimatter associated with this statement.

Refinement sessions do not include planning; they groom the product backlog. It is recommended that the development team can spend a maximum of 10% of their capacity for product backlog refinement activities. We should concentrate on giving our user stories a better shape regarding details, clarity, conditions of satisfaction, size, and so on. If we conduct a planning session during this meeting, we will start the next sprint, in the middle of the current sprint. This is not the right time to plan the next sprint. This is to create inputs for the next sprint planning.

We conduct sprint planning in the last responsible moment (LRM), that is, just before we start working on that sprint. The value archived in the current sprint is an input for the next sprint planning. As work progresses in the current sprint, many aspects can change at every moment. The priorities will change, product backlog emerges, current state of the product changes, and sprint retrospect will produce actions that we have to accommodate. Considering all these factors and dependencies, Scrum defines the best sequences for its events.

Sprint planning is not only about identifying the backlog items for the next sprint. The team and Product Owner decide on the expectations from the upcoming sprint. This will result in a sprint goal. The development teams will discuss about how they are going to work as a self-managed team to achieve this sprint goal. The sprint backlog will be created and activities for the first few days will be identified. If we avoid this meeting or dilute its relevance, we will end up on the losing side. Sprint planning or any other prescribed timeboxed event has a reason and has to be conducted at the right time in the correct sequence.

15. Develop in Cadence

A Scrum Master's life is full of challenges. He has to step into different roles according to the work demands: a servant leader, a passionate coach, an effective change agent; the list is endless. He has to safeguard Scrum and ensure that the team enacts it. He has to assist the team in reaching that perfect rhythm and maintain it indefinitely. Many external factors will be present that disturb the cadence in which the team operates. The team delivers in cadence and over a period reaches optimal productivity that can be maintained indefinitely. The Scrum Master should be alert to identify and prevent any disturbances that might occur during this smooth transition.

The team has to handle many strange requests. I remember an interesting proposal. The team was running four-week iterations. It was about to start working on a new capability that needed more than one sprint to complete. An interesting statement was made during the sprint planning.

"I don't mind you extending this sprint for another week. I can't wait till the completion of the next sprint for this."

This posed many questions. Can we change the sprint duration for a sprint? When should we end one sprint?

I remember the early days of a team where it usually extended the sprint until it completed all of the work scheduled for that sprint. This is a wrong practice. The guidance is extremely simple and straightforward. The sprint ends when the timebox expires. There is no doubt about this. In addition, a new sprint begins on the next day. This is irrespective of whether we complete the work scheduled for the sprint.

Why is it so dramatic? The sprint itself is a timeboxed event that contains many other timeboxed events. The team should work in a rhythm, which helps it to produce better results. We know that a planning meeting is held every alternate Monday at 10 AM, a sprint retrospective is held every alternate Friday at 2 PM, and so on. Any temporary changes or adjustments will impact this rhythm and brings in more predictability and helps the teams in self-organization.

How will we address such demands from the business particularly when we have long sprints? Scrum doesn't mention that all the items selected for the sprint should be completed only in the last week of the sprint. We can concentrate on the low hanging fruits or high priority items early in the sprint. When the item is potentially shippable, it is up to the Product Owner to decide when to ship it. He doesn't have to wait until the end of the sprint to do this. However, keep in mind that a certain level of automation will help this to happen smoothly, or we should be in a framework where development is not affected by the deployment tasks.

16. Coaching on the Job

What is the best way of adding a new Scrum team to an existing project? How do we induct it into the existing organization? It was a medium-sized project where two Scrum teams operated from the offshore development center. It was decided that one more team should be added to the project. Eight new members were recruited and were all set to join the project.

"So we have eight new faces. Let them work with the existing teams for a couple of sprints. After that they will break from them and form a new team." The management voice sounded a bit odd again. The intention was to expose the new team to the project so that they can be productive once they start working.

Does this sound good? Will it disturb the existing teams? Yes, it will. Team membership can be changed with a short-term impact on productivity. However, what should be the ideal team size? Scrum recommends teams with three to nine members. If the size increases, it will create exponential increase in the coordination efforts. The communication becomes more complex and productivity will suffer. It is a common theory that adding more people beyond a certain level will not bring in expected increase in productivity.

How should we address this situation? We should provide basic training to the team members and kick-start the new team at the earliest. Let the team learn practically. It can reserve some time in the initial sprints to observe the tasks performed by the existing teams. This will not impact the existing cadence and gives the new members an opportunity to learn the best practices followed by the existing teams.

However, this has another aspect. Handholding with the existing teams and osmotic transfer of knowledge will not be optimal as it is across team boundaries. We can think of other alternatives such as restructuring the teams to include new and existing members in all three teams. This should be done with a proper analysis to minimize the movements and impact. This will ensure that the new members are inducted and become productive at the earliest. However, this comes with a cost. The existing rhythm will be temporarily affected and there will be an impact on productivity till the teams get back its rhythm.

17. The Long Review

"We will continue the meeting post lunch; there are many items left to be discussed."

The team was in the middle of a sprint review meeting with an extended audience. It was running two-week sprints. This time it had several user interface (UI) intensive features to demonstrate and was unable to end the meeting on time. Therefore, they decided to extend it further.

Is this a good practice? No prize for guessing the answer as sprint review is a timeboxed event. The duration of the meeting is four hours if the sprint is one-month long. Therefore, for two-week sprints, it should not exceed two hours. Is this the only concern with the preceding example? We can read more in to it.

Why do we conduct a sprint review? A sprint review is a meeting where the Scrum team and other stakeholders collaborate on the current state of the product and discuss the way forward. It is an inspect and adapt event. However, many times it is observed that the sprint reviews are hijacked by the product demo. Of course, a demo of the increments produced by the team is an important part of the sprint review. It enhances the opportunities for direct feedback and encourages discussion on how we should proceed further. But a sprint review is much more than a product demo.

The Product Owner discusses the current state of product backlog and speculates regarding the future based on current velocity. The participants discuss the current state of the product and product backlog. This will result in further improvements to the product backlog and provide directions for future sprint planning. Product demo is an important item, but it is not the only one item in the agenda for the review meeting. The demo should facilitate further discussions.

It is the Scrum Master's responsibility to coach the team to restrict the sprint review within the timebox. The team should make wise decisions regarding the items to be demonstrated. It should prioritize the items so that it doesn't miss the opportunity for direct feedback.

18. A Fancy Sprint

"I don't find any release sprint in this plan. Are we missing something?" A debatable topic was coming to limelight. Tighten your seat belts; we are landing on a controversial topic. What is a release sprint? Do we need one? Is it in line with Scrum principles?

A release sprint, also known as a hardening sprint, is a sprint defined toward the end of a release timebox. For example, you will have six development sprints, followed by a release sprint of the same duration. During this time, the team prepares the product for release and rolls out. There are any benefits explained by the promoters of release sprints.

Some experts think that a difference exists between potentially shippable and shippable increments. Scrum is intended to produce a potentially shippable product increment. They feel that we need a release sprint to execute the final round of testing in real environments, which is expensive to do at every sprint. This may lead to further fine-tuning of the product. Is this in line with Scrum? With due respect to all experts, I prefer to stay away from this argument.

Here, we are addressing the wrong problem by using a release sprint. The problem at hand is that of a testing infrastructure. We should ensure that at least our staging environment is in sync with the targeted environment. We should explore different options available today including simulators that can help us. The term "potentially shippable" doesn't dilute any quality expectations from the increment. It should be ready for shipment in all aspects. The only factor that remains should be the decision on the shipment time and the activities required for shipment. We should pay serious attention to the automation aspects. An automated test suite and build deployment scripts will help in improving these activities.

It is a crime to conduct a release sprint to accommodate all leftover items from previous sprints. This is no parking lot for such garbage; it should be cleared then and there. Every sprint produces a shippable increment. Let's not define any additional parking lot that will take us away from the core values of Scrum. Every sprint is expected to produce a shippable increment of the product. Introducing special sprint with names such as release, hardening, or sprint0 will impact this rhythm and is against the basic principles of Scrum.

19. It is not a Silver Bullet

Many myths and misunderstandings surround Scrum. Some of them are because of a lack of understanding of agile and Scrum and others are intentionally put in place to justify some practices. For example, we hear people say why are you documenting; Scrum doesn't need documents, and you should concentrate only on development. Another myth is that Scrum leads to chaos as there is no proper planning and therefore, I don't like Scrum.

Is Scrum against documentation? The Agile Manifesto states that we value working software over comprehensive documentation. It states that documentation has value, but we value working software more. Agile is not totally against documentation. It has a value, but in agile we give more value to working software. We need just sufficient documentation. We should allow the code to talk for itself as much as possible. The intention of this guideline is to avoid unnecessary documentation that doesn't add value or, which is just a duplication of information, which is available in some other part. For example, if the logic is very clearly visible in the code, why do we need a separate document to represent the same?

Is Scrum against plans? I feel we plan more in Scrum. But we do just enough and at the Last Responsible Moment. We have plans at different levels, from the product vision to the daily plan. We have release, sprint, and daily plans. However, here the major difference is that we have a high-level plan for a long period and a detailed plan for a short period.

All these are common myths about agile. I remember another interesting discussion that took place a few months ago. The team was having a technical discussion with one of the architects. He was not a member of the Scrum team, but used to serve as a consultant for the team for technical concerns. They were trying to make a design decision. Toward the end, they narrowed down to two alternatives. It was a tradeoff as both had their own merits and drawbacks.

The architect comes up with an idea. "What does Scrum recommends, Option A or B? Why can't you call up your agile coach?"

Does Scrum tell you how to code a particular module? It doesn't. Scrum gives you a better framework where you can employ different engineering techniques. It doesn't give you an engineering solution for your problem. It gives you a framework where the design evolves along with the product. It suggests technical excellence and flexibility for your designs. But it doesn't give an algorithm for selecting a design over another. It is up to the team to select what is best for the situation.

20. Single Neck, But All Responsible

I was returning from office after a busy day. While driving back, I received a call from my Product Owner.

"I have sent you three new user stories that we have to consider high priority."

"What do you want me to do with that?" I was fighting the traffic and that reflected in my voice as well.

"We have to add them as priority items in the backlog. At the same time we have to consider the existing items as well."

"OK, well, please proceed. I guess we have a Product Owner to do all that." The traffic was really getting into my mind.

I was partially wrong here, and I lost control over my words. Luckily, before it was too late, I realized my mistake and brought the relationship back to normal. However, I felt this topic needed some more discussion. What are the responsibilities of each role with respect to maintaining product backlog?

A single neck, that is the Product Owner, holds all matters related to the business value of the work that the team does. How does he ensure that the team is working on the right items? He ensures this by maintaining the product backlog according to business priorities and clearly communicating the same to the team. He is the single source of requirements for the team and has complete authority over the product backlog. The entire organization respects his decisions regarding the product backlog and its ordering. But this doesn't allow others to take their hands off from the activities related to the product backlog.

The development team should assist the Product Owner in maintaining the product backlog. They can spend a maximum of 10% of their time for these activities. This helps in different ways. The Product Owner receives assistance and more importantly, the development team gets an opportunity to understand the backlog items better. One of the most effective ways for the development team to understand the items is to work with the Product Owner in refining them. A well-refined item in the product backlog has a size associated with it. This size should come from those who are actually implementing that item. This is another reason for the development team to get involved in backlog refinement activities.

What will be the role of the Scrum Master here? In simple words, he ensures that all the aforementioned activities occur. He helps the Product Owner in coordinating with the team for refinement. He coaches the Product Owner and the development team to refine the items. He helps the Product Owner, with appropriate techniques to prioritize the items. He helps the Product Owner in finding right techniques for maintaining product backlog. He ensures that all understand the relevance of a well-maintained product backlog.

21. Welcoming the Changes

When we go through the Agile Manifesto and its principles, we can find many remarks regarding the ability to respond to changes. Agile manifesto says *"Responding to change over following a plan"*

In addition, the second principle states *"Welcome changing requirements, even late in development. Agile processes harness change for the customer's competitive advantage."*

How does Scrum implement these? Can we change the requirements at any point of time? We have seen how requirements are being added to the sprint backlog through the sprint planning session. However, if the requirements keep on changing, won't it lead to chaos?

I remember a scenario where one of the stakeholders proposed some major enhancements to an item, which was under development. The development team went back to the Product Owner to keep that user story open for another sprint to accommodate the new changes. The Product Owner rejected the request and asked the team to concentrate on what was originally committed. He took the correct decision. Many times we have discussed that the Product Owner should be a single point of contact for the team on requirements. So let's not touch on that point again.

Till what time can we accept changes in the requirement? The answer is at any point of time; but there is a check point, that is, the sprint planning meeting. During this meeting, we decide on what we are going to work on during the next sprint. Once it is decided, the new changes have to wait till the next sprint planning to be considered for development. It doesn't mean that the requirements cannot be changed during the sprint. The Product Owner can continue updating the product backlog. However, the items that are selected for the sprint should remain intact. The new changes or enhancements should be entered as separate items in the product backlog.

So generally, we can say that the requirements should remain unchanged within a sprint. It is usually said that we should select the sprint duration in such a way that we can keep the selected requirements unchanged for that duration.

Can we stop this discussion with this statement? There are a few more points to discuss. Even within the sprint, we can welcome changes if they will not reduce the chances of achieving the sprint goal and if they are acceptable for both the development team and the Product Owner. Is that all? No, at any point of time the development team can renegotiate the scope with the Product Owner if there is a genuine reason for that. . The sprint is closed for changes from outside. But the development team and Product Owner can discuss the scope even within the sprint keeping the sprint goals in mind.

22. The Hierarchical View

A customer visit was organized in one of the offshore development centers. The account manager was introducing the visitors to the team. First, they were introduced to the project manager, who handled that particular engagement. Then, they were introduced to the quality manager who was responsible for quality standards and processes. Next, they were introduced to the test manager who led the testing team. Then, they were introduced to different module leads. At this time one of the visitors turned back and asked "Who does the development here? Do we have someone who does the work?"

The comment was in a lighter vein and everyone laughed. It was a traditional project organization and this implementation was part of the system. We have observed many times that such an organization influences the Scrum implementations as well. I remember a Scrum team, not sure if I can call it by that name, yet to come out of this traditional hierarchy. They had renamed the roles to give it a Scrum flavor. However, business was as usual. It was a distributed team in an onsite-offshore model. It included a Product Owner, technical owner, and quality owner, working from the onsite. The Scrum Master, team lead, test lead, and development team were working from the offshore development center. This structure was repeated in every team.

Scrum doesn't recommend any roles other than Scrum Master, Product Owner, and development team. All other roles are introduced to the structure because of many reasons such as organizational processes; workaround solutions to problems, which are not properly analyzed; historical reasons; and political environment. All these come with a cost. I remember the team running around for approvals toward the end of the sprint. The increment that the team produces has to be accepted or rejected by the Product Owner. However, in the above scenario it has to be done from the quality owner, technical owner, and the Product

Owner. This happens at every stage of development and not only with acceptance. It may bring in some benefits but at the cost of Scrum.

It is not a rigid hierarchy; it is a self-organizing team with better engineering practices that brings in quality. Along with the Product Owner, the team decides and brings in the quality gates as required for the product.

23. It Evolves

"We can't take up any more stories related to this functionality. It is a high priority, but unless the communication infrastructure is in place, we can't move forward."

The team was developing a customer registration module. The minimal marketable feature included email communication and notifications. There was another team working on the communication infrastructure. It included many features apart from email. It planned to release the first set of features in the next two sprints. In other words, we can say that there was an unresolved dependency.

How should we handle such dependencies? How should we handle the infrastructure? Why can't we wait until the complete infrastructure is in place before we start developing features? All these dependencies should be identified and the work should be sequenced at different levels of planning. Regardless of the infrastructure being developed by the same team or a different team, it evolves along with the product itself. We talk about the enough design or the design that evolves. The same is applicable for infrastructure.

What went wrong in the above situation? When we say a detailed plan for a short duration at the Last Responsible Moment, it doesn't mean that we should not look forward. There should be enough forward thinking with whatever details available to us at the given time. Here the coordination between different teams should be observed. The dependencies are not considered while planning the work. The minimal marketable features and release plans of the infrastructure team could have been in sync with the requirements of the larger program. They could have redefined the plan and created a small roll out for the email capability. The feature team could have synced with the infrastructure team much earlier. The grooming sessions could have found out such dependencies and tracked them before we move the story to the ready for implementation state.

What is the best way of addressing such dependencies? Different flavors of a scaling framework come in to the picture here. Depending on our situation, we can opt for complicated frameworks such as scaled agile or think of conducting simple Scrum-of-Scrum meetings.

24. Inside the Timebox

Once again let's get inside the magic box. What does timeboxing mean? Is it the average or minimum time that an activity can take? Or should the activity take exactly the same time? If an activity takes exactly the same time, is it 100% efficient?

In Scrum, timeboxing denotes the maximum time an event can take. It is set when we begin our sprints. Scrum recommends timeboxes for its events. For example, we have an eight-hour sprint planning session for a month-long sprint. If we are unable to complete it in time, it indicates some other concerns in the team, such as the backlog items may not be in a ready state, the team may not be concentrating on the task, and the Scrum Master might have failed to teach the team on efficient planning.

Another example can be a daily scrum that runs beyond 15 minutes. If we analyze, we can find real concerns such as long technical discussions being held during the daily scrum, team members not joining on time, the meeting diverting toward other topics, concerns with infrastructure, and tasks of other events creeping into the daily scrum. So timeboxing helps to identify such concerns and enables us to address them as early as possible.

I remember a four-hour planning meeting conducted for a two-week sprint. The team was able to accomplish the goal in 3 hours. It had decided on the items for the sprint. The sprint goal was finalized. It had decided how it was going to work in this sprint and listed down the activities for the initial days. The Scrum Master had a wrong perception of timeboxing.

"Guys, we have another hour to go. We have two options; we will come out with a report on the expected task distribution across different engineering areas for the next sprint. It will give us a picture of where our efforts are concentrated."

What should we do if we have achieved the goals before the timebox? That's simple; close the event and start working on the sprint activities. We should not conduct any unnecessary activities just because we have time. Doing this has two basic concerns. Most of the times we will work on tasks that will be considered waste, such as the report in the preceding example. Another problem is that it creates new precedence that we will be forced to work on again. This is applicable in any framework and not only with Scrum. If we start a new practice because we have some additional time, people will start expecting it the next time onward and we will be forced to provide it.

25. Rules of the Day

We will review the smallest but most frequent prescribed event, the daily scrum. This time, we have an interesting Product Owner.

"Most of the items are clear to me," the Product Owner kick-starts the daily scrum. "I am missing inputs from Marc and John. If they can update their status quickly, there is another topic that I have to update you all with."

I know you might have thought of reprimanding me for bringing back this topic. However, trust me this is something that has occurred. This is the simplest event, and simultaneously the most difficult one to practice. It is only for 15 minutes and the agenda is also extremely simple. However, this is the event where we can find majority of the problems.

Let me share another instance to add to the drama. The team is working in the offshore development center in Bangalore and their Product Owner is working from Seattle. They are working in different time zones. The daily scrum is scheduled for 10 PM, Bangalore time, so that the Product Owner can participate. As it happens, after office hours, all team members in Bangalore log in to a voice bridge for the scrum call. In addition, more interestingly, all the team members start sharing their updates addressing the Product Owner.

The daily scrum is a timeboxed event of the development team, for the development team, and by the development team. Many times it is hijacked by other roles. In the first scenario, the Product Owner takes it as a meeting to note the status. For him, it is a status meeting. He fails to understand its value. It is an inspect and adapt meeting for the team. Each member reflects on what they have done since the last meeting, what are they going to do until the next meeting, and are there any concerns involved in achieving the sprint goal. What really happens here is daily planning. The team collaborates and discusses how it is proceeding toward the sprint goal. The three questions give a framework for achieving this. This is not a status meeting for the

Product Owner or Scrum Master; it is for the team. Each member shares his updates with the team.

The second scenario is also around the same point. The team conducts the daily scrum at night, beyond working hours, which is not the ideal time for the meeting. Timings should be such that face-to-face conversations are maximized. The best time to conduct this meeting is toward the start of the day.

This is a meeting for the development team to synchronize and plan for the next 24 hours. The Scrum Master ensures that it happens and teaches the team to timebox it to 15 minutes. He ensures that all team members actively participate in this event.

26. Track Them to Closure

Whenever there is a discussion on Scrum Master responsibilities, the word impediment takes a center stage. We are always taught that one of the main responsibilities of the Scrum Master is to handle the impediments to ensure that there are no blockers for the team. At the same time, we talk a lot about self-organizing teams. How can both these concepts go hand in hand?

The team is facing an impediment. It has no good quality test data to test the increments. The available test data base is outdated and it creates concerns when they deploy their product increments. So the team has to put in additional efforts to correct the issues that come up during deployment. This has risen as a major impediment. The Scrum Master doesn't have a magic stick to create data from thin air. He has raised this concern with the Product Owner. He has agreed to get the representative test data from the business and add a high priority item in the backlog to update the test data based on the sample.

On another day, the team was struggling with their communication infrastructure. It was working in an onsite-offshore model and did not have sufficient licenses for initiating video calls. The Scrum Master stepped in and implemented an effective pooling system with available licenses. In addition, he had arranged for a few new licenses.

The first step in handling impediments is to identify them proactively. I don't want to put this responsibility on the Scrum Master's shoulders; it is a team work. The team should consider all aspects that may come in its way in achieving the sprint goals. Second, we should track the impediments to a solution. The team should maintain a list of active impediments and update it with a required frequency. We can consider this as one of the possible outputs from the daily scrum. The impediment list should contain enough details to track it. At the same time, it should not become bulky with irrelevant information.

The third step is the solution. Who should resolve the

impediment? In our first example, the impediment resolved once the team completed the backlog item for creating the test data. Therefore, the solution was offered by the team. The Product Owner and Scrum Master play different roles in making it happen. In the second example, better organization within the team and support from the performing organization keeps the problem under control.

Again the role of the Scrum Master is that of a facilitator. He ensures that the impediments are resolved. It is done with the help of the team, Product Owner, organization, and so on. The Scrum Master coordinates with all required stakeholders to get the problems solved.

27. One Product, Many Teams

"Why are they doing this?" A few of the team members were a little disappointed. "We were working on this module for many sprints. We were all set to take the new story in the next sprint. But now it is given to some other team." They were thinking within the team boundaries and failed to understand the situation.

How do we work in a scaled environment where more than one team works on the same product? A few of the main areas of concern were maintaining a single product backlog and making it available for multiple teams. First, let us see how the situation will look like. There will be a Product Owner for each team; more precisely there will be only one Product Owner for a team. This is in line with the theory that there should be only one point of contact. However, a Product Owner may be assigned to more than one team. There will be more than one Product Owner for the product. Does it appear a little confusing? It is a complex scenario; we must draw a diagram to understand this.

As per the guidelines, a single product should have a single product backlog, irrespective of the number of teams working on it. Now, how will we make these items available for multiple teams? How can we distribute this among different teams? In this scenario, many implementations come in to the picture and new roles, such as chief production owner, enter the stage. Let's not get in to the specifics of these frameworks. What matters most in the present situation is the coordination within the group of Product Owners.

All Product Owners contribute to a single product backlog and all teams pull out stories from the same product backlog. We can expect the Product Owners to align among themselves with implementation of concepts such as chief Product Owner, Product Owner round table, requirement workshops, and so on. But when we consider the development teams, the number of heads involved will be multiplied on an average by eight and coordination will become demanding. We need some broker mechanism between the master product backlog and individual Scrum teams.

The solution can vary from a simple team tagging done within the master product backlog to maintaining team specific backlog views. Regardless of the implementation, the single source should be the master product backlog. The team-specific views should be present only for making team-specific planning sessions more effective. It should be ensured that no one perceives team backlog views as a separate entity with an independent existence. These are only pointers to the master list.

The pointers are not tightly bound to a team. In our example, the Product Owners decided to change the team tagging for an item so that it was delivered in the current sprint itself. There is nothing wrong with this move. The Product Owners should rearrange these views as and when required without impacting the cadence with which the teams are working.

28. The Hard Nuts to Crack

Scrum depends on self-organizing teams to deliver value, sprint after sprint. These teams comprise individuals from different backgrounds. They have different personalities, personal interests, and more importantly, different ways of working. The success of the team depends on how well the team overcomes these boundaries and strikes a balance. Many times, ground rules help in maintaining decorum and enhancing the opportunities for team work.

Sam was a member in one of the Scrum teams working out of an offshore development center. There was no question about his technical capabilities and he maintained a good relationship with other team members. However, the team felt that something was missing between him and the team and that was his way of working.

He was a regular at team events and participated actively in them. He attended the daily scrums, shared his updates, and voiced his concerns. He was active in the refinement sessions. He worked on his tasks with full commitment. I guess we should read the last sentence again: he worked on his tasks with full commitment. He was committed only to his work and not to the team. He was present for all scheduled events, but he used to leave the office after that for his personal work. He used to return in the evening and stay back late in the night and does his work. The team might have already left for the day by that time. What is wrong here? He does his work, contributes in all prescribed events, and the team is not blocked because of him. What else he should do?

He was unable to give his best to the team, because his work timing was not in sync with the team's work timing. As stated before, Scrum is all about team work. It is the team that commits and delivers, and it is the team, and not an individual, that succeeds or fails. He may complete his work, but he was not working in a team. He will be able to perform well if he works in the team. Agile values individuals and interactions more than processes. A major part of the communication occurs in an osmotic way. For this to happen there should be sufficient sync time for the team. For a team to commit and deliver a piece of work successfully, all team members should be committed to the sprint goal. Even when we are working in distributed teams, we should ensure that there is sufficient overlap time available for the team members.

29. The Daily 'Sit Up'

The daily scrum is extremely critical for sprint success. It gives the team the chance to inspect and adapt on a daily basis. Like a flight control system, it is useful in analyzing our progress toward the goals and realigning ourselves to the target. It improves the chances of achieving the sprint goal. Many times, daily scrum is referred to as daily stand up. It is good to be a stand-up meeting, but there is no strict recommendation as such. Any specific instances are not discussed in this session. We will try to collect a few observations from the daily scrums.

Our team decided to conduct daily scrums sitting around a long elliptical table. Everything went well during the initial days. But later, as the sprint progressed, a few concerns arose. A few of the team members used their mobile phones during the daily scrum. They shared updates when it was their turn and went back to using their mobile phones.

Scrum promotes individual interactions and face-to-face conversations, but we must control them during the daily scrum. Team members developed the habit of having parallel discussions while the daily scrum was in progress. As they were sitting on movable chairs, it was easy for them to turn around and start a conversation with the person seated next to them. It was not easily noticed as the table was long and elliptical.

As it was a distributed team, two members joined the Scrum through voice. An Internet phone was placed on the table. Team members developed a habit of talking to the phone. They kept looking only at the phone while talking, even though the majority of the team was present in the same room. In another version of this problem, team members had a tendency to talk to the Scrum Master rather than updating the entire team.

How can we improve this situation? The human mind is disturbed very easily. So we should minimize the factors that impact their concentration. The best way to conduct a daily scrum is by making the team stand around facing each other. This will help the team to concentrate more. As we are facing the entire group and not seated in our chairs, the chances of cross talks are less. We will learn to address the entire team when we are in this position.

Daily scrum is the shortest prescribed event. A small disturbance will impact the outcome of the event. Every minute is important and we have to use it to the maximum benefit.

30. Inspect to Adapt

We conducted all prescribed events religiously, in a timeboxed way, with a correct agenda. In addition, we followed the right sequence as well. Are we done? Does this ensure that the events meet their goals? One aspect that we often miss is maintaining the connections among these events. A sprint review provides inputs for the planning and product backlog. The sprint provides inputs for review and retrospect. The retrospect provides inputs for the next planning and upcoming sprints. All these are connected with each other. One of the main links that we often miss is the one connecting retrospect.

We conduct retrospect and come up with action points. However, how often are these considered in our planning meeting? Many times with new teams, the sprint retrospect becomes a standalone event. We conduct the retrospect, document the output, and leave it as it is. Most probably the same items will figure in the next retrospect as well.

I remember a team claiming that this time it had an extremely effective retrospect. I asked the team what made it think like this.

"The team was participating with full mind. We are able to find 25 valid points and action items against it."

I asked the team "What is the current velocity of the team? How much have you committed for the current sprint?"

They were surprised as if he heard an irrelevant question. "It is around 45 and we are forecasting the same."

Here lies the problem. Retrospect is an inspect and adapt event. The team reflects on the previous sprint and suggests ideas to make future sprints more effective and enjoyable. However, this inspection warrants adaptation that doesn't come for free. An effort is required for adapting the suggested changes. Results from the retrospect should influence the upcoming planning sessions. If required, the action items may be added to the sprint backlog in one form or other. It may even introduce new items in the product backlog.

Now, how do we balance these? We should run our normal

activities that produce the product increment. We can't dedicate the entire sprint in handling retrospect points. The answer is simple: opt for prioritization. Instead of acting on all the items that come up in retrospect, select a few (two or three) top items. Devise a plan for it and address it in the next sprint. Consider the effort required for this during planning and ensure that these actions are part of the sprint backlog if required. If they are not part of the sprint backlog, track them separately till the solution.

31. The Sustainable Pace

Whenever we talk about the productivity of Scrum teams, the first word that comes to our mind is velocity. It is nothing but the number of story points achieved by the team per sprint. It is the total number of points assigned to stories that reached the done criteria in the sprint. It serves as an indicator for the amount of work that the team can take up in upcoming sprints. It helps in forecasting possible burn down of the product backlog in future. However, all these predictions are based on available data. For each sprint, the user stories are different, and there will be changes that impact the productivity of the teams. It is just an indicator and we should understand that when reading the team velocity.

Current velocity is an input for sprint planning. How do we calculate velocity for the team? There is no single answer for that. The teams follow different methods. Some teams take the average of the last three or eight sprints. Other teams consider the best three or worst three out of the last eight sprints. We can also choose the last sprint velocity. The method is decided by the team based on project specific considerations. Regardless of the method, it is an indicator of the team capacity.

At the same time, velocity is an aspect often misused. I came across a strange project plan where they assumed a steady increase in velocity by 10% every sprint. Can we increase velocity indefinitely? This is similar to filing marbles in a container. Instead of marbles, let's take small objects of different shapes and sizes. The total mass that we can accommodate in the container will keep increasing during each attempt. Our expertise will increase and we will arrange objects in an optimal way so that we can accommodate the maximum number of objects. In this process, we will try many options including cutting the objects in to small pieces. However, to what extent can we improve? We will keep improving till we reach an optimal level. From there, we will continue to give that output as long as the size of the container remains the same.

The same is true for team velocity. We will keep improving the output as we become more and more organized and experienced. Using this process, the team should reach a sustainable optimal level. The term sustainable is very important. We may be able to increase our velocity by subjecting ourselves to more pressure. But it will not be sustainable. Our aim should be to sustain the good momentum than increasing it indefinitely. The agile principle states that *"Agile processes promote sustainable development. The sponsors, developers, and users should be able to maintain a constant pace indefinitely."*

32.   The Strict Scrum Master

Agile values individuals and interactions more than processes and tools. This statement can be applicable to the processes defined by different flavors of agile as well. Scrum has various prescribed events. All of these events have specific goals to achieve. At the same time, it provides space for the team's creativity.

Scrum defines sprints of short duration, but it is up to the team to decide on the engineering practices to be followed during this period. Scrum demands the prioritized product backlog, but how to prioritize is left up to the practitioners. If we think on these lines, we observe that in the case of the daily scrum, Scrum takes an additional step. It defines the agenda regarding three questions that the team has to answer.

What did I do yesterday that helped the development team meet the sprint goal?

What will I do today to help the development team meet the sprint goal?

Do I see any impediment that prevents me or the development team from meeting the sprint goal?

I have worked with a Scrum Master who was extremely strict on this. He raised alarms the moment any member deviated from this agenda. He claimed to be a strict follower of the process and didn't allow even a small technical discussion during the daily scrum. He raised the alarm even when someone asked a quick question. Do we need events to be this dramatic? How much flexibility can we have in daily scrums?

First, we should understand the purpose of the daily scrum. The daily scrum is a 15-minute timeboxed event where the development team collaborates and creates a plan for the day. It analyzes the work that it has done since the last daily scrum and decides on what should be done until the next daily scrum. The three questions give it a framework to achieve this goal.

What we have to concentrate on here is the timebox and goal of the meeting. As long as we achieve the goal within the timebox,

I personally feel that a minor tailoring can be accommodated. There is no doubt that we should avoid long technical discussions and problem solving in this meeting. But there is nothing wrong in asking quick questions and providing clarifications on the fly. This should not lead to a situation where all team members do not get time to reflect. Fifteen minutes and three questions are time-tested solutions and we should stick to that. Within these boundaries, it is up to the development team members to define what works best for them.

33. Automate to Enable

Scrum concentrates on creating the best possible value for the end user. All sprints create product increment. In short, we can say that all activities are aligned toward creating value. Citing all the aforementioned reasons, a team member asked the following question.

"Why do we automate our test cases? The test automation code that we produce is of no value to the end user. Is this as per Scrum?"

The answer is simple here. The sprint goal is to produce the product increment and any activity that helps the team in achieving this is a valid activity in the sprint. This doesn't mean that we can dedicate a sprint for test automation. The automation should be carried out in parallel with other activities. Like the requirements, design, and code, the automation code also evolves. How far should we automate? I feel as much as possible. One hundred percent automated test cases will be an ideal case, but require higher investments. Therefore, the team should decide the extent of automation.

Automation is not limited to the test cases. An ideal environment will have automated build and deployment infrastructure as well. Then the build will be triggered the moment the developer submits a change. This will in turn start the automated test cases. Once these steps are successful, deployment scripts will deploy the latest version of the product in a specific environment. In addition, the latest deployment files will be made available at a centralized place for any developer to access and update his individual machine.

What are the benefits that automation brings in? It saves time and eliminates human error that may occur while repeating the steps manually. These are the direct benefits for any type of automation. Automation has many indirect benefits. The automated build and test infrastructures will enable the team to maintain a green baseline at any point of time. A fine-tuned system can ensure that the code will be entered into the system only if it doesn't break the existing system. This helps in maintaining green-to-green baseline changes. The product can be deployed at any time with a few clicks. As it is automated, any team member will be able to perform any of these tasks: testing, build, or deployment. This enhances the cross-functioning abilities within the team.

34.   Start Creating Value

"It is a long-term project. Perform a detailed requirement analysis during the first two sprints."

The Scrum Master tried to convince the stakeholder about the way the requirements were being handled in Scrum. The stakeholder had agreed to them, but kept offering the same suggestions.

"Let the requirements evolve. We don't introduce any requirement freeze, but we will spend a couple of sprints on requirements so that we get an overall picture and can have a better plan."

When should we begin development in Scrum? Should we conduct an initial requirements sprint? The goal of each sprint is to create a potentially shippable product increment. Scrum doesn't recommend any special type of sprint for requirements or design. Only one type of sprint is the one provides value to the customer. Therefore, we should start sprinting as early as possible.

But when will we develop the requirements? How can we proceed without requirements? Requirements are developed in parallel with the development sprints. When the development team works on a particular sprint, the requirements are refined for future sprints. This will have other benefits as well. It will be easy for the stakeholders to express future requirements as they have one version of the working product. They will be able to think in a more structured way and communicate their requirement more precisely.

What will happen if we start with a new project? How can we start? There should be an initial set of requirements for the team to start. There are many ways of addressing this. The Product Owner can groom some requirements to be almost ready before the first sprint so that the team can deliver an increment from the first sprint onwards. The team and the Product Owner will complete the remaining refinement of the user story and develop it within the sprint. They will groom stories for the upcoming sprints simultaneously.

During the initial sprints, more effort may be expended toward refinement activities. This doesn't mean that we are dedicating a sprint for requirements. For every sprint, the goal is to create a product increment. This will help the team in achieving rhythm at the earliest and also help stakeholders to express requirements more effectively

35. The Process Web

"How will this be added to the acceptance criteria?" The developer raised a concern. "This is an item related to performance. This has nothing to do with functionality."

Let us consider another scenario. The Scrum Master is suggesting an additional item in the acceptance criteria. "All code changes should be checked in to the "xy.z" version." This is a requirement of the quality processes of the company. All the teams should follow this process. The Scrum Master wants to track this item and he feels the acceptance criteria would be an ideal place to do it.

One of the best ways of tracking performance requirements is to add them as part of the Definition of Done. This is true with any nonfunctional requirement, which has a system-wide impact. Many times it will be difficult to handle the performance requirements separately as a different user story. It will not only impact the features that are currently being developed, but also the upcoming stories. So there is nothing wrong in adding them as a part of the definition of done.

The point raised in the second example is related more to the Definition of Done (DoD) than the acceptance criteria. It is not related to functionality or system characteristics. It is all about process adherence and coding discipline. We can add it as a part of the DoD. Organizational processes are among the sources for the items in the DoD. Different guidelines will be followed in the performing organization. These have to be followed by the delivery teams, but don't have any direct connection with the product under development.

Handling these kinds of existing processes will be a two-step approach. First, we have to check if it adds any If it is just an overhead, we should negotiate with the concerned parties and try to modify the processes. Next, the team should decide where to track it. DoD need not be an automatic selection. Sometimes we should handle it separately also. The team will decide the best place for it on a case-to-case basis.

36. Bring Them Together

How important is colocation for a Scrum team? Can the team work from different locations? Here, we cannot give a single answer. If we go by the word, the team has to be collocated. Scrum depends on the self-organizing and collaborating nature of the teams. To enhance this ability, the team should sit and work together. But to what extent is it possible in the current situation? Does it create hurdles in today's global work environment? Talent will be distributed across different locations. The same will be the case with opportunities. Any method that operates in this environment should be flexible enough.

Scrum recommends collocated teams. But how we implement this colocation depends on the environment. Team members can be physically present in different locations and still work as a single team. This has to be achieved by effectively employing infrastructure support and carefully putting down ground rules. An example of the required infrastructure can be a video presence system for daily scrum and a ground rule can ensure that team members are present in time for the event.

The distribution of team roles also plays an important role. I was associated with a distributed team of nine members. Three of them including the Scrum Master were working from a different location. One item that kept repeating in their retrospect was regarding handling of impediments. It used to take many forms. Sometimes it took the form of delay in getting infrastructure support or dependencies remaining unresolved. The core concern was that impediments were not being tracked effectively. The team was able to improve the situation to some extent by using physical information radiators.

However, the root cause of the issue remained unsolved. The Scrum Master was not present with the majority of the team. Technology can help us in being virtually together, but it cannot replace physical presence and face-to-face interactions. So our first priority should be to bring the team together at the same location. If it is not easy, try to make it possible at the earliest. If it is not possible at all, take the help of technology and try to improve collaboration. Remember this will not be as effective as physical presence and there will be many concerns associated with it. So put in additional efforts in identifying and resolving the concerns at the earliest.

37. Are We Full?

"Are we full?" The Scrum Coach kept asking the team after every story. The planning session was in progress. The team was discussing the stories one by one. The Scrum Coach was assisting the team as he found areas of improvement. After committing each story, the team was asked this question to ensure that there was space for more stories. The exercise continued and the team was not showing any signs of saying "No."

"What is your current velocity?" The Scrum Coach realized it is time to intervene.

It was around 40 story points.

"How much have you committed so far?" The team had already taken up stories amounting to 50 story points and was still ready to take more.

Further analysis revealed the real reason. Another team working on the same project was maintaining a velocity of 50 and this team didn't want to be behind. It was ready to take up additional work above its capacity to match these figures. It might have been disturbed by some passive comments from some corner and has started comparing itself with the other team.

This is a situation that can be observed in many teams. May be the wrong perceptions about Scrum existing in the organization makes the teams start these comparisons. But what is wrong with these? The teams worked on the same project. They created increments for the same product and shared the same product backlog. Positive steps were taken to bring in parity in the estimates across the teams. So can we use velocity to compare team performances? Regardless of the arguments supporting it, I will never prefer to compare the team performances based on velocity. Each team is different and the work it does is different. What is the benefit or value expected out of these comparisons? I am unable to find any use of it, other than creating unhealthy competition.

The comparison should be made between sprints for the same team. We can compare the velocities of the same team in different sprints. This will give us an indication as how the team is progressing as a self-organizing team. We can track its progress toward reaching desired levels of productivity. Any variations will enable us to analyze the concerns and address them sooner than later.

38. Sizing the Slices

How big is a story point for you? This is an extremely old question that keeps repeating. I don't know the answer. I am not worried about it as well. I will be able to forecast the number of story points that my team may finish in a sprint. This is based on previous experience. We can tell a user story is an eight pointer comparing it with other stories. Still, what does one story point mean? I prefer to leave that question unanswered.

Let me change the question a little. How will you decide the size of your first story in your first planning poker session? Again, I will escape this question by saying it will be a subjective decision based on previous experiences of the team and it will be a reference for further estimates. Let me close all the loopholes. It is a new team and it is performing the estimation for the first time. Here, we have to determine the reference point. We can proceed in two ways. The team can select a story, which is relatively of a small size and assign a point by planning poker. We can try to find a story, which can be considered a one or two pointer. In both cases, we are not trying to equate it to hours.

There is another practice followed in many teams. For the first time, the team will consider certain effort in hours and try to find a story, which can be completed in those hours. It will consider the story to be an "n" pointer. For example, the team will take 16 hours and find a story that can be completed using that effort and mention it as a two pointer. They claim that they will forget the calculation by hour and going forward estimate based on comparison. There is a danger here. It is extremely difficult for humans to forget this measurement, especially when we try to forget it intentionally. Every time team members try to make a relative estimate, the hourly estimates will be dominant in their minds. They may not state it explicitly, but internally a re-estimate will take place for each story instead of a comparison.

Let's keep the absolute estimation out of our mind and make a relative estimation while sizing the user stories. We don't need an absolute value. We are not using these values for comparison between teams. We use it just for planning at different levels. As these are relative estimates, we can use them irrespective of the environment.

39. The Single Neck to Hold

"I am sorry. You have delivered a lot, but it doesn't give me the confidence with the current state of the product. The main features that we are looking for are yet to be started."

These were the words of the customer in the first monthly project review meeting. The team had successfully completed five two-week sprints and was maintaining a good velocity as well. It was the first time that the customers were reviewing the emerging product. This is something that had taken place a few months before with one of the teams new to agile.

Whenever it is about the right business direction and the value of increments from the team, there is only a single neck to hold, the Product Owner. It is one of the major drawbacks of Scrum as well. What went wrong in the above scenario? We can find many areas for improvement. All reasons will point to the same root cause: lack of collaboration between the Product Owner and the end customers.

Something was missing with the prioritization of the product backlog. Either the customer failed to invest enough time with the Product Owner or the Product Owner failed to use the available time. In both cases, the Product Owner had failed to do a proper prioritization.

There were no frequent interactions with the customer. Why should we wait for two months to get a feedback from the customer? The Product Owner should ensure there are frequent feedbacks from the customer on the product under development. The best way is to invite the customer for product demos. If it is not possible, the product owner should take the product to the customers for their feedback. This can also be done offline in an asynchronous mode.

The bottom line is that all stakeholders should constantly interact at a desired frequency. This will bring in more transparency and facilitate fast and consistent feedback.

40. Apples and Oranges

It was the day of the sprint retrospect. The Scrum Master got a call from one of the stakeholders. He wanted a particular topic to be discussed in the retrospect. He felt that the output from the team was below expectations. He compared the team's velocity with that of another team and observed that our current velocity was much lower. The other team was working on the same technology and had the same strength. So he wanted the team to discuss this point. The Scrum Master was not really convinced with his argument. However, he decided to discuss this point.

During the retrospect, as a coincidence, the same topic was introduced in a different form. The team members were complaining about the way the story points were assigned. The stories that could be developed in a few hours had a higher number than those that took five days to develop. During the last sprint planning, the team members were unable to commit as per the current velocity. When they discussed the selected items, it was observed that more effort was required than expected. In short, the velocity did not serve as a good indicator for the future.

The team was working in an offshore development center. There were teams working in parallel at the onsite. User stories were estimated by teams available at the onsite. This was done because of some agreement in the project. The team was not complaining about the number. It was fine with the numbers as it understood that these were relative estimates. It was worried about the consistency, which has two aspects: consistency while comparing the stories and consistency while estimating at different times. They wanted stories of the same size to get similar numbers within the sprint and across different sprints.

What can be the best way to address this situation? No prizes for guessing the answer. The estimation should be done by the team who does the work. This is the best way to make that estimation and will give the best estimates. It will bring more consistency to the estimates as the same team is making the estimates over and over again. It makes the sprints more predictable. It has another indirect benefit. It will improve the chances for the team to have more clarity on the story.

The answer was more straightforward in the first scenario. The story points were not for comparing between the teams. What a story point means to one team will be totally different from what it means to another team. It will be similar to comparing apples to oranges. Story points and velocity can be used for tracking the team's progress toward a sustainable optimal level and how they consistently achieve it.

41. Are We Done?

"What all do you want me to do?" The production owner expressed his disagreement. The team was in their initial days of Scrum just like the Product Owner and was trying to finalize the Definition of Done (DoD) with the Product Owner.

"We all are on the same page regarding user stories. The acceptance criteria are clear and agreed upon. Then why do you need another layer?" He was under the impression that we were duplicating information. He felt that we were creating unnecessary documentation.

"What I need, I have written in the story. I need only that."
A serious misunderstanding exists between conditions of satisfaction, that is, the acceptance criteria and the DoD. The acceptance criteria express the conditions to check if the increment is developed as per the requirement. It checks if the requirement is converted into the working software correctly. But can we say we are done with the user story once it satisfies the acceptance criteria? The team has put forward this question to the Product Owner.

"Yes, I am happy if it is working fine in the staging environment and user documents are updated in draft."

The Product Owner has answered with a yes, but simultaneously he adds two more conditions in addition to the acceptance criteria: the increment is available in the staging environment and the user documents should be updated in draft. This list won't end here. We have to perform many other tasks. These tasks may come from different sources including the quality process followed in the performing organization. They may be in the form of some specific quality gates during testing. They can be coding disciplines like the code has to be reviewed and checked in a specific branch. There can be some legal aspects that the increment has to manage. DoD has a higher scope compared to acceptance criteria. The DoD informs when the work is completed for an item in all aspects. This is decided and agreed with the Product Owner at the time of planning and can be defined at different levels, which are user story, sprint, and release levels.

42. Inbuilt Performance

"As a user of the portal, I want all pages to be loaded in 6 seconds or less."

The user story was extremely clear for the team and all stakeholders. This is a valid requirement. It is achievable and testable. However, will it make a good item to work on? How do we estimate this item? This is applicable for any page that we are developing for the product and for all the pages in future. This is a characteristic of the entire application. How do we handle the nonfunctional requirements in Scrum?

The preceding story was proposed to a team, which had started the development of a new portal. Different ways were used for handling these kinds of requirements in the teams. Sometimes these requirements take the form of a user story. This is good if we can define the requirement within sufficiently small boundaries. For example, if the nonfunctional requirement is specific to a process or a page, we can handle it extremely well, just like a normal user story. If the user wants to receive a confirmation of his order within a given time frame, we can opt for a user story. This is a performance concern, but it is still specific to a process, which can achieve its done criteria independently.

However, consider the case of our first example. This has an impact on the entire application as it grows. We cannot reach a done state until we finish developing the application. We know the product backlog exists till the product exists. New pages can come up at any time and those pages have to adhere to this condition. So this is an ongoing process. This aspect should be taken care of while making any additions to the product. How do we handle this? There are two aspects to this. First, the Product Owner should have a mechanism to record and communicate this requirement. Then, there should be a mechanism to validate this consistently. One way of addressing this concern is by adding it to the definition of done for related user stories. In the preceding example, any UI related user stories should have this concern as one of the items in the definition of done.

It is up to the Scrum team to decide what suits it best for the given requirement. This has no single correct answer. The team should consider various aspects of recording, communicating, and validating these requirements and should select the best approach on a case-to-case basis. It can be a user story, an item in acceptance criteria, part of DoD, and so on.

43. Break the Wall, don't Just Move

An example is often used to criticize the traditional software development. It is called throwing requirements over the fence. Requirements are thrown over the wall to the development team. The development team develops the product and throws it back. What is the result? The developed product may not be what is actually required by the end users. Scrum addresses this concern by bringing in opportunities of close collaboration among all parties. The agile principle states *"Business people and developers must work together daily throughout the project."*

Customers become part of the development process. They see the system getting developed. This will foster opportunities for early and continual feedback. Another benefit is that there will be more transparency. Everyone shares the same information regarding progress and is aware of how the work is progressing toward a usable product. Therefore, the wall between the development team and customers has become extremely thin and transparent, if not completely removed.

However, some teams still have a traditional mindset. They tend to keep the Product Owner on the other side of the wall. I happened to overhear a conversation in a team area. The predictions that the team members made during the planning had gone wrong. They had actually overcommitted well over their capacity. They were reluctant to return to the Product Owner and discuss with him as they felt it will give a wrong image about the team. They were planning to stretch their time and complete the work as committed. In short, they had decided to hide the current situation and opt for workarounds.

This is a dangerous situation. It is against the very basic pillar of Scrum called transparency. Scrum a separate role called Product Owner. This doesn't mean that the development team has to maintain a distance from him. He is part of the Scrum team and the Scrum team should work together on a daily basis. The

Product Owner should be aware of occurrences in the team.

While implementing Scrum in traditional environments, a dedicated effort should be devoted toward bringing in the highest levels of transparency and collaboration. This will be one of the toughest tasks for the coach and Scrum Master. There should be continuous efforts from both, the development team and the Product Owner, to achieve this.

44. The Gatekeeper

"So we will finish the small items first," the manager was interfering again. "We can attack the low hanging fruits first. It will give a better picture right from the early days."

The Scrum Master had to request for a meeting with the manager to make him understand how Scrum works. He tried to convince him that they should allow the team to suggest the best way to sprint.

"Do you mean to say that we should let them do whatever they want? Where is the control? We have years of experience and we can tell them how to proceed. What is wrong in making use of our experience?"

He was not done with his arguments.

"At the end of the day it will be you and me who are answerable. So we should be in control."

There were many arguments to defend his stand. I am sure you might have faced at least one of these if you have practiced Scrum for a few years.

Who has the authority to decide how should we sprint? There is no doubt that it should be the development team. The Product Owner tells the team what it should do and the Scrum Master coaches it on how to work as a self-managed team. However, it is the Scrum team who has the final say in how it is going to complete the work. During the sprint planning, the development team creates the sprint backlog and explains the Product Owner and the Scrum Master how it is going to work as a team to achieve the sprint goal.

Another point in the preceding discussion was regarding control. Who should control the work? How should we bring in control? A self-managed team controls and manages itself. In Scrum, the aspects of control are inbuilt. It is a collaborative work. The Product Owner controls the requirements regarding their value and priority. The development team controls the development process that includes completing a part of work. Timeboxed events control day-to-day activities. We plan in short durations and this keeps the risk under control. Scrum provides many opportunities to inspect and adapt. Transparency is one of the pillars on which Scrum is built.

Will this prevent the team from making use of the experience and knowledge available in the organization? Scrum doesn't prevent the development team from taking external advice, but the final decision should be taken by the team. Scrum doesn't prevent me from giving a valuable suggestion to a Scrum team, but I should not break in to the daily scrum for that. I should convey it at the right time through the right person. For example, if I feel the team should be taking up items in a different order to maximize the business value, I should put it to the Product Owner.

45. The Cadence

"Why do you keep worrying about these small things? Please concentrate on the main job."

This is the reply that the Scrum Master received when he requested for a permanent room for the Scrum team. The manager continued. "This is a knowledge industry. We are dealing with people and not machines and rooms. You can use the rooms as and when they are available."

The team was having difficulties in getting rooms for its events. It used to have the daily scrum at different places as per availability. Many times it had to reschedule events as rooms were unavailable. Team members carrying big Kanban boards between rooms has become a usual scene. Is this a major concern? Can't we live with this?

Let's see what will be an ideal scenario. I will opt for a team space, a scrum room, which is exclusively for the team. This room has a common space where the team sits together. This will optimize collaboration and osmotic communication. The team won't have to run around for space. It can keep all physical information radiators here. Anyone who enters this team space can understand the current situation. At the same time, there should be provisions for private spaces. There will be activities that the team member has to do individually without many disturbances. We can define the entire space with a common collaboration area in the middle and individual workspaces around it. It is just a matter of turning the chair toward the center to get in to a quick meeting.

Another important aspect is the event timing. Scrum recommends that the daily scrum should be conducted at the same time and place. This will remove numerous overheads in organizing the meeting. Apart from every team member, the entire organization will know that this team is having its daily scrum at 10 AM in its team space. This makes life much easier. Anyone who wants to be there can plan their day accordingly. The same can be applied for other events as well. It is easier to remember that the sprint planning is conducted every alternate Monday at 10 AM in the same room. The same will be the case with retrospective, review, or even no prescribed events such as refinement sessions. This brings in better rhythm and the team doesn't have to spend much effort in arranging these.

46. The Relay Race

This is something that happened a few hours before I wrote these lines. I was invited to attend a presentation on Scrum implementation in a software project. My friend told me that it was something different and they were implementing a new model. Yes, it was totally different from my expectations, but I was reluctant to call it Scrum.

The team was trying to implement Scrum in a product enhancement project where the requirements are changes and enhancements. The sprints were one week long. They had defined an end-to-end workflow that consisted of designing, development, testing, and deployment. Each of these phases had separate teams. Any change that enters the system will have a design sprint followed by development and testing sprints, before it reaches the deployment team. They called it Scrum.

Scrum is not a relay race where we implement a design sprint, development sprint, and so on. Many times, we tend to do a waterfall within the sprints. Here, let's go back to the basics. The goal of a sprint is to produce a potentially shippable increment of the product. We develop this increment within the sprint. It involves design, development, testing, and deployment. Instead of dedicating separate teams or separate sprints for these processes, the development team does a little of all these activities every sprint. It will pick a backlog item, design it sufficiently, develop it, test it, and keep it ready for a potential shipment.

It is proven beyond doubt that Scrum is an efficient way of developing software. This doesn't mean that it is the only good framework existing in the world. Many frameworks exist within and outside the agile umbrella. It is up to the stakeholders to choose what works best for them. They should be aware about the best practices available in each environment and should take expert help in making a selection. Scrum need not be an answer for all problems. We should not opt for Scrum just because the term is attractive and very hot in the market.

47.   Enough and Effective

A lot of discussions are taking place on tracking the sprint progress. Should it be based on tasks or fine-grained user stories? How should we collect and maintain this information? Let's keep these aside and look into another aspect of it. Where should we maintain it?

Let's consider an example of a distributed team of nine members. Three of the members were working from a different location and had good infrastructure support. Each member was equipped with video call facilities and other communication channels. The members used collaboration tools effectively. They were in a dedicated team area with video conferencing facilities. In short, all the team members were virtually close to each other.

The team was using one of the best online tools for managing Scrum projects. All the artifacts were created and maintained in the tool. Sprint backlog was maintained and tracked using this tool and it provided many views including burn downs. All those who needed an update could log in to it and view the progress. For every sprint, after the planning, the team used to take a printout of the user stories and tasks from the tool and put it on a Kanban board displayed in its team area. The team used to update it every day during the daily scrum.

The story does not end here. The team used to maintain a physical burn down chart in its room. It used to calculate and update the remaining work after every daily scrum. I wish I could stop here. But there is one more thing. Apart from all these things, the Scrum Master took a screenshot of the burn down and sent it to a distribution list every day. This is not a fictional story. This is a real-life example from one of the teams that I incidentally interacted with. It was hard to believe for me till I witnessed the scene.

This is an example of overdoing things. The same piece of information is repeated at four places. This happens even when it is available for all at a centralized location. We should avoid such duplication as effort is wasted and focus is diverted away from the sprint tasks. It is a good idea to keep physical information radiators, but we should keep only the minimum required radiators. I prefer to maintain a single location for tracking and making available to all stakeholders at a centralized location. We should opt for a pull communication here. The information is available at a centralized location and everyone can pull the information they want from this location.

48. Timeboxed, but

Don't think that I hate managers, heads, and so on. On the contrary, I always had a good relationship with them. I am lucky to have been associated with some great personalities. I remember working with an extremely supportive center head. She was ready to do whatever she could for the team. She understood what was happening at ground zero but never micromanaged. She trusted her team and provided them with the required freedom.

I was working with a Scrum team for an internal project. The center head was overseeing this project from a management perspective. During that time, one of our sprints ran into trouble. Three out of six members in the team had to take emergency leaves for medical reasons. We were on the third day of the two-week sprint. These three members were going to be on leave for at least one week. So the result was that the sprint goal was in danger.

"It is unfortunate and this is something that we cannot plan for." The helping hands appeared for our support.

"How long will it take to complete the committed work with the available team?"

I did not think about the implications of that question and gave a quick reply. "I guess it will take up to an additional week."

She made some calculations in her mind and offered a suggestion.

"One week, I am not sure. We will extend the sprint by three days and give it a try."

She offered this suggestion because of her lack of experience with agile projects. I was able to make her understand what was missing in this suggestion and how we should handle this situation. The problem with her proposal was clearly evident. The sprints should end when the timebox expires. They should not be extended as we wish. Work remains in a sprint don't make a reason for its extension.

How can we come out of this situation? The key roles here are of the team and Product Owner. The capacity of the team had reduced unexpectedly. Now the sprint goal and commitments had to be renegotiated with the Product Owner. The Product Owner, based on business priorities, guides the team.

In traditional development, the scope is fixed, whereas time and cost will vary. However, here the time was fixed and the scope varied. Within the available time, we estimate the best we could deliver with the expected quality.

49.   The Daily Reports

"Are you in control?" Once again the Scrum Master faced the heat.

"Yes, the sprint is on and we don't have any major impediments," the Scrum Master replied.

"But it is not visible in your burn down. Why is it not updated on a daily basis?" Before the Scrum Master could explain further, the task was assigned.

"Now onwards, by the end of the day, please update the burn down and drop me a mail."

How important is the burn down chart? What is the best way to track progress? Here, we are referring to the sprint burn down chart. It represents the total amount of work remaining in a sprint at a given point of time. Why should we maintain it? It is an information radiator. It is a pictorial representation of our progress toward completing the identified work in the sprint. I prefer to use the term identified work. As we start with the activities, new tasks may come up. Therefore, the burn down can turn in to a burn up temporarily and we cannot ensure that once we finish all the remaining work in the burn down, we will achieve the sprint goal. We can make it more predictive if we use fine-grained user stories and burn down based on user stories.

In summary, we can say that sprint burn down reflects the progress within the sprint. This is not only for the development team. We can make it visible for all stakeholders. As it is visible for all, we can avoid many other reports.

What is the best tool for the development team to track the progress toward the sprint goal? I will say it is the daily interactions. This is my opinion and I am not sure if all agree to it. The development team collaborates to inspect the current state and adapt in a way that maximizes the chances of achieving the sprint goal. Burn down is a great tool, but there is a limit to represent the status in black and white. Another important artifact is the impediment list. The team identifies and tracks the possible threats to the sprint goal using this list. If this list is maintained religiously and the items in it are in control, we can say that there is a good probability of achieving the sprint goal.

When should we update all these information items? All these inputs can come up at any time during the day. Many teams make it a practice to update these soon after or just before the daily scrum. If we are using some tools, such as a Kanban board, it will be a good idea to update it during the daily scrum. We can move around the items as we share our updates.

The most important point that we have to remember is that all these tools are enablers enhancing the probability of achieving the sprint goal. They should not create burdens or roadblocks in our ways.

50. Agile Myths

Scrum is a lightweight framework that is easy to understand but difficult to master. We have to break many myths in our journey of understanding Scrum to mastering it. I used to start the agile induction session by asking the participants about their perceptions on agile. Many interesting thoughts were shared.

Agile means no documentation. This is the most common myth regarding agile and Scrum and has made it the top spot in the myth list. On the contrary, this myth attracts many people to agile; many core technical minds are interested in this. Agile doesn't mean zero documentation. It gives more importance to the working software and simultaneously acknowledges the importance of adequate documentation. We should restrict the documentation to a sufficient quantity, which can be easily maintained and let the code do the talking, as much as possible.

Agile means no planning, which is the second myth in the myth list. According to this myth, we should start working and shouldn't waste time in planning. However, I feel the other way. I think in Scrum, we plan more, but in small amounts. We have a detailed plan for the sprint and high-level plans for release, product, and so on. We don't create a detailed plan for a long term as we don't have enough visibility of the future and our intent is to accommodate changes even at later stages. We conduct a high-level prediction for the long term and create a detailed plan for the immediate future. We plan at different levels.

Scrum delivers the product quickly, does it? I am not sure of the source for this thought. Consider a traditional team that works in an ideal scenario at high level of productivity. How can we say that Scrum can make them faster? Instead of that, I prefer to say that Scrum can deliver the most important functionality faster. This is because we prioritize the product backlog as per the business requirements. In addition, we are able to accommodate the changes proposed by the business more effectively. This will also reduce waste. Studies show that a huge percentage of features present in any software application, are rarely or never used. Prioritization allows Scrum teams to take up these low priority items for development only towards the end or never. Agile principles state

"Deliver working software frequently, from a couple of weeks to a couple of months, with a preference to the shorter timescale".

All these make the features with highest priority available for the end users at the earliest.

Many other myths exist at different levels. All these myths exist because of a lack of understanding or partial understanding of the Scrum framework. A better understanding of the framework and knowledge that comes from (our or other's) experience will help people in debunking these myths.

End Notes

A lot of interesting incidents can be recollected from our experience with Scrum, which leads us to some learning and a better understanding of Scrum. This book attempted to discuss a few scenarios that I have personally encountered while working with different Scrum teams. We have tried to analyze them within the Scrum framework. Scrum is a lightweight framework that is easy to understand but difficult to master. The best way to learn Scrum is by practicing it.

Let's sprint.

www.ingramcontent.com/pod-product-compliance
Lightning Source LLC
Chambersburg PA
CBHW031225050326
40689CB00009B/1471